Desert Biome

by Grace Hansen

Abdo
BIOMES
Kids

abdopublishing.com

Published by Abdo Kids, a division of ABDO, PO Box 398166, Minneapolis, Minnesota 55439.

Copyright © 2017 by Abdo Consulting Group, Inc. International copyrights reserved in all countries. No part of this book may be reproduced in any form without written permission from the publisher.

Printed in the United States of America, North Mankato, Minnesota.

052016

092016

 THIS BOOK CONTAINS RECYCLED MATERIALS

Photo Credits: AP Images, iStock, Shutterstock

Production Contributors: Teddy Borth, Jennie Forsberg, Grace Hansen

Design Contributors: Laura Mitchell, Dorothy Toth

Cataloging-in-Publication Data

Names: Hansen, Grace, author.

Title: Desert biome / by Grace Hansen.

Description: Minneapolis, MN : Abdo Kids, [2017] | Series: Biomes |
     Includes bibliographical references and index.

Identifiers: LCCN 2015959086 | ISBN 9781680805000 (lib. bdg.) |
     ISBN 9781680805567 (ebook) | ISBN 9781680806120 (Read-to-me ebook)

Subjects: LCSH: Desert ecology--Juvenile literature.

Classification: DDC 577.54--dc23

LC record available at http://lccn.loc.gov/2015959086

Table of Contents

What is a Biome?. 4

Desert Biomes 6

Plants. 16

Animals 18

Things You Might See
in a Desert Biome 22

Glossary 23

Index 24

Abdo Kids Code. 24

What is a Biome?

A biome is a large area. It has certain plants and animals. It also has a certain **climate**.

desert

forest

freshwater

marine

grassland

tundra

5

Desert Biomes

Deserts are the driest of all biomes. They get lots of sunlight. They get very little rainfall.

There are four main desert biomes. Hot and dry deserts are hot all year long. They are extra hot in the summer. Rain is rare.

9

Semiarid deserts are hot, too. But they have clear season changes. Summers are hot and dry. Winters bring a little bit of rain.

Coastal deserts get a bit more rainfall than others. The summers are warm. The winters are cool. More animals live in coastal deserts.

13

Cold deserts have cold and snowy winters. The winters are long. The summers are short. So, it is cool and dry most of the year.

Plants

Special plants grow in deserts. Cacti are common. They store water in their stems and leaves. They have wax on them. The wax keeps water from **escaping**.

16

17

Animals

Only certain animals can live in deserts. **Reptiles**, such as lizards and snakes, live in deserts. Rodents live in deserts, too. They dig holes to stay cool.

19

Large **mammals** rarely live in deserts. However, camels have **adapted** to desert life. They can go a long time without food or water. Their humps store fat. Their stomachs store water.

21

Things You Might See in a Desert Biome

animals

horned lizard

roadrunner

tarantula

plants

barrel cactus

desert marigold

prickly pear cactus

22

Glossary

adapt – to change something so that it is easier to live in a certain place.

climate – weather conditions that are usual in an area over a long period of time.

coastal – the land along or near the ocean.

escaping – getting out of.

mammal – an animal that feeds milk to its young and usually has hair or fur covering most of its skin.

reptile – a cold-blooded animal that lays eggs and has a body covered in scales or hard plates.

Index

animal 4, 12, 18, 20

climate 4, 6, 8

coastal desert 12

cold desert 14

hot and dry desert 8

mammal 20

plant 4, 16

rain 6, 8, 10, 12

reptile 18

rodent 18

season 8, 10, 12, 14

semiarid 10

abdokids.com

Use this code to log on to abdokids.com and access crafts, games, videos, and more!

Abdo Kids Code:
BDK5000